Jason Alisa

Regain Her Trust

10 Healthy ways to build lost trust; Tips on how to win back trust from your wife, girlfriend and friends.

Copyright © 2022 by Jason Alisa

All rights reserved. No part of this publication may be reproduced, stored or transmitted in any form or by any means, electronic, mechanical, photocopying, recording, scanning, or otherwise without written permission from the publisher. It is illegal to copy this book, post it to a website, or distribute it by any other means without permission.

First edition

This book was professionally typeset on Reedsy
Find out more at reedsy.com

Contents

1. What in all actuality does trust truly mean 1
What trust really means, and what it closely resembles in the extent of a relationship. 1
Indications of trust in a relationship 1
It's likewise vital to comprehend what trust isn't. 1
2. How trust can be broken in a relationship 4
Trust in a relationship can be broken by the accompanying: 4
3. Could trust be rebuilt 6
4. 10 Moves toward Remaking Trust in Your Relationship 8
Own up to your role 8
5. Straightforwardly apologize 10
6. Request a great chance to talk 12
7. Acknowledge liability 14
8. Effectively tune in 15
9. Back up your words with actions 17
10. Consider the experience 19
Commit to clear communication 19
11. Reignite the connections 21
Add the component of secret or shock. 21
12. Make New Recollections 23
Use your abilities 23
13. Spotlight on what's to come 25
14. Revamping trust as the person in question 26
15. Potentially inquiries of the casualty wrongdoer 30

16. The bottom line..32
17. Mostly asked questions...33
   1.
      1.
      2.
      3.
   2.
      1.
   3.
   4.
      1.
   5.
   6.
   7.
   8.
   9.
   10.
      1.
   11.
      1.
   12.
      1.
   13.
   14.
   15.

16.

1

What in all actuality does trust truly mean

As the familiar aphorism goes, trust is the underpinning of each and every relationship, except that trust can, tragically, be broken. To begin, it very well may be useful to consider trust a decision that somebody needs to make. You can't make somebody trust you. You probably won't decide to believe somebody until they show that they deserve it.

What trust really means, and what it closely resembles in the extent of a relationship.

Beauchamp depicts it as a sensation of responsibility and confidence — similar to a major, warm embrace. "Trust has a real sense of reassurance, agreeable, and secure," she says. "You feel like you can reliably depend and rely upon your partner in the midst of hardship. Regardless of what is up in the air, you have a protected establishment and some place to land."

Indications of trust in a relationship

Trust can mean various things to various individuals. In a close connection, trust could mean:

You feel committed to the relationship and to your partner.

You feel safe with your partner and know they'll respect physical and emotional boundaries.

You know your partner listens when you communicate your needs and feelings.

You don't feel the need to hide things from your partner.

You and your partner respect each other.

You can be vulnerable together.

You support each other.

It's likewise vital to comprehend what trust isn't.

In a relationship, for instance, trust doesn't guaranteed to mean you tell your partner each and every thing that enters your thoughts. It's absolutely commonplace to have individual considerations you mind your own business.

Trust likewise doesn't mean giving each other admittance to:

financial balances (except if it's a common one)
- Personal computer
- cells phone
- online entertainment accounts

You may wouldn't fret sharing this data, particularly in the event of a crisis. Be that as it may, the presence of confidence in a relationship by and large means you don't have to determine the status of your partner. You have confidence in them and feel ready to discuss any worries you could have.

2

How trust can be broken in a relationship

Frequently that is because of disloyalty, and different times it's a consequence of one partner accomplishing something that double-crosses the other accomplice's feeling of safety and certainty. Trust can likewise be broken when any sort of assumption in a relationship isn't met, says Antoinette Beauchamp, ensured proficient holistic mentor. This frequently turns into the case on the grounds that these assumptions sadly are not generally spoken with the other individual, and subsequently, lines get crossed.

A great many people view trust as the critical calculate to a solid relationship. It's expected to be defenseless, form associations, and keep a feeling that everything is safe and secure. Sound connections are based on trustworthiness, or doing what you say you will do. At the point when this isn't respected, the well being, certainty, and backing of a safe relationship is obliterated, for a brief time.

Trust in a relationship can be broken by the accompanying:

Not faithfully keeping a word

Not assuming a sense of ownership with unforgivable way of behaving

Keeping love as well as warmth

Absence of physical or close to home closeness

Habit-forming ways of behaving (i.e., drugs, liquor, porn, gambling)

Betrayal (both a sexual and nonsexual issue)

Being straightforwardly condemned or your partner talking brutally about you despite your good faith

Hitting a close to home "crude spot".

3

Could trust be rebuilt

The way to fixing broken trust is figuring out how to discuss the issue in a manner that makes a shared comprehension of what happened — where the two sides can discuss the episode in a genuine and blunt way. At the point when accomplices can discuss the issue and put each of their interests on the table, it permits couples to make an arrangement for fixing the harm done. With the right information and abilities, broken trust doesn't need to prompt a descending winding of put in a bad mood, pessimism, and more double-crossings, however it gives couples the chance to take care of through issues and make their relationship more grounded simultaneously.

How individuals approach an accomplice when a double-crossing becomes visible has all of the effect on the planet. Standing up to an accomplice in a threatening and accusatory way generally prompts a cautious reaction where issues seldom get examined or settled.

It assists with moving toward one's join forces with a useful, helpful mentality when a selling out becomes exposed. Taking on a helpful methodology makes it more straightforward for couples to have real conversations and track down arrangements, if any exist. A helpful, productive methodology includes discussing one's sentiments in a manner that makes sympathy as opposed to a cautious response ("I'm so sorry" versus "How is it that you could do this to me?").

Moving toward the treachery valuable is just the first of many advances that couples need to take to fix broken trust.

Trust is a fundamental part of areas of strength, however it doesn't occur rapidly. Furthermore, whenever it's wrecked, it's difficult to reconstruct.

4

10 Moves toward Remaking Trust in Your Relationship

Reconstructing trust in your relationship can be troublesome after it has been broken or compromised. Contingent upon the idea of the offense, persuading your accomplice that you can be relied upon again may try and feel unimaginable. The uplifting news is, Trust can as a matter of fact, be remade in the event that the two accomplices will invest the effort and work.

Any solid relationship is based on an underpinning of shared trust. Contingent upon the conditions encompassing a break of trust, the means for repayment might shift.

These steps below serve as a basic outline for reparation.

Own up to your role

Assuming you have insulted or harmed somebody by breaking trust, it's basic to think about your activities and recognize and possess your job. Excusing, avoiding, limiting, or projecting fault won't help you in that frame of mind to understand what occurred and pursue fix. You should possess your part to yourself before you can persuade your accomplice you have taken proprietorship. Put your walls down and your inner self to the side," Beauchamp says. "Weakness welcomes weakness and increments closeness. Making close minutes will help support and modify which is wrecked."

5

Straightforwardly apologize

Straightforwardly apologize

For some individuals, saying 'sorry' doesn't come without any problem. Remaking trust requires an exceptionally sincere statement of regret. Be deliberate about pushing ahead with your conciliatory sentiment "While it very well may be simple for the individual who broke their accomplice's trust to be protective, this just irritates the misery in the relationship," Cook says. "Whether it's a letter, a significant discussion, various discussions, or one more method for communicating a statement of regret, it's critical that the individual communicates regret and a longing to fix the relationship." In the event that you lied, cheated, or generally harmed your accomplice's confidence in you, a certified expression of remorse is an effective method for beginning setting things straight. It's vital to recognize you committed an error. Be explicit, when you apologize, be well defined for show you understand what you did was off-base. Use "I" articulations. Try not to put fault on your partner.

For instance, rather than "Please accept my apologies I hurt you," attempt:

"Please accept my apologies I misled you about where I was going. I realize I ought to have been come clean with you, and I lament causing you torment. I maintain that you should realize I'll at absolutely no point ever do it in the future."

Try to follow up by letting them know how you mean to try not to mess up the same way once more. On the off chance that you don't know what they need from you to chip away at the relationship, you can inquire. Simply ensure you're prepared to pay attention to their response effectively.

Simply recollect that your conciliatory sentiment isn't an ideal opportunity to legitimize your activities or make sense of the circumstance. Assuming a few variables impacted your activities, you can continuously share these with your accomplice in the wake of saying 'sorry' and possessing what is going on.

6

Request a great chance to talk

Request a great chance to talk

The maxim "timing is everything" can have an effect while saying 'sorry' Ask your accomplice when a great opportunity to talk would be. Tell them you have something significant you might want to examine. Allow them to direct the planning of that conversation so they can give it, and you, their full attention.Give your accomplice time

Regardless of whether you're prepared to apologize, discuss what occurred, and start managing things, your accomplice may not feel prepared at this point. It can require investment to find some peace with a selling out or broken trust.

Individuals process things in various ways, as well. Your accomplice should talk immediately. In any case, they additionally could require days or weeks before they can resolve the issue with you.

Allow their necessities to direct you

Your accomplice might require existence before they can talk about what occurred. What's more, frequently, this could include actual space.

This may be hard to confront, however regarding your accomplice's limits and needs can go quite far toward showing them they can rely upon you once more.

Your accomplice might need additional straightforwardness and correspondence from you later on. This is normal after a treachery of trust. You might try and enthusiastically share your telephone and PC with your accomplice to demonstrate your trustworthiness.

Be that as it may, on the off chance that you've gained some headway in fixing your relationship and your accomplice keeps on checking your exercises and correspondences with others, conversing with a couples guide can help. It's essential to try not to constrain them to have a conversation before they're prepared. Apologize and tell your accomplice you're prepared when they are. In the event that you're battling meanwhile, consider conversing with a proposition fair and strong advisor direction.

7

Acknowledge liability

Acknowledge liability

.You have previously taken ownership of yourself. Presently it is the ideal time to show your accomplice that you acknowledge liability. Be genuine and use "I" messages: "I am so sorry to have harmed you," "I truly care about you and feel horrible that I have let you down." Be explicit, while conceivable, with respect to what you are heartbroken about: "I am so sorry I let you know that I went to the store when I was entirely else," "I feel dreadful that I misled you about how I spent that cash." Convey that you need to make things right. Tell your accomplice you perceive that you broke their trust and you will make a solid effort to recover it. Additionally, perceive that being sorry doesn't mean whipping yourself. Nobody is great, and no one's perfect. Assume liability yet be caring to yourself. It is typical to encounter some culpability, disgrace, or self-hatred; simply don't allow it to overpower you. View at this as a chance to develop and to make your relationship more grounded.

8

Effectively tune in

Effectively **Tune in**

Undivided attention is an example of listening that keeps you drew in with your partner in a positive way. It is the most common way of listening mindfully while another person talks, summarizing and reflecting back the thing is said, and keeping judgment and counsel.

Focus completely on the thing is being said. Tune in with every one of your faculties and concentrate on the speaker. Set aside your telephone, overlook interruptions, abstain from fantasizing, and shut down your inward exchange.

To show the individual you're really tuned in, take a gander at them and be aware of nonverbal ways of behaving. Utilize open, harmless non-verbal communication. Try not to overlap your arms. Grin, incline in, and gesture at key crossroads. Intentionally control your looks, staying away from any that convey bad introductions.

Visually connecting is particularly significant. As a rule, intend to keep up with it for 60% to 70% of the time you burn through tuning in

In the wake of saying 'sorry' listen to your partner. You've spoken; presently it is the ideal time to tune in. This implies being responsive verbally as well as with your non-verbal communication also. I know feelings might be increased, yours notwithstanding. Remain even-tempered and approve your partners sentiments; they reserve an option to them.

9

Back up your words with actions

Back up your words with actions

A certifiable expression of remorse is off the charts valuable. Notwithstanding, without any completion, your words become insignificant and future endeavors at fix might be dismissed. In the event that your conciliatory sentiment is acknowledged, it ultimately depends on you to show an example of reliable conduct over the long haul. Go all the way and focus on being the best version of yourself: be modest, be caring, be warm, be thankful, be faithful, be cherishing, and be dependable. It is valid, individuals might stand by listening to what you say, however what you do is more significant than your words. We ordinarily realize this illustration right off the bat throughout everyday life. At the point when we hear a parent first express, do as I express, not as I do, we realize something isn't exactly correct.

Before somebody can acquire our trust, their activities should match their words. After all, who wants to be around people they don't trust? Are you building trust through your words and actions? Are you sure?

10

Consider the experience

Consider the experience

To restore trust in the relationship, the two accomplices should likewise find opportunity to introspect, check their close to home space, and concentrate an example from the experience. "Invest energy thinking about what it is that caused you or your accomplice torment," Beauchamp says. "Think about the activities taken that broke the trust in any case. What did it cause you to feel? How can you feel now because of all that occurred?"

Commit to clear communication

In the quick fallout of broken trust, you'll need to genuinely address your accomplice's inquiries and focus on being totally open with them later on.

To do this, you need to ensure you're sure about the degree of correspondence they need.

Suppose you broke their trust by keeping some data you didn't believe was truly significant, and you didn't see the reason why they felt so double-crossed. This can demonstrate there's a more profound issue with correspondence in your relationship.

To fix your relationship and try not to hurt your accomplice again later on, you want to arrive at a common comprehension of what great correspondence resembles.

Miscommunications or misconceptions can here and there cause as much torment as deliberate deceptive nature.

11

Reignite the connections

Reignite the connections

Rather than review broken trust as a relationship hindrance, consider it a chance for a new beginning. Beauchamp recommends utilizing this chance to revive the fire among you and your partner. One method for doing this is to get familiar with one another main avenue for affection (love languages) and deliberately giving each other what is vital to feel completely cherished, safe, and upheld in the relationship.

Add the component of secret or shock.

Both secret and shock likewise emulate the close to home condition of another sentiment. In any case, it doesn't mean whisking your partner away to the Mediterranean or astounding your better half with thousand-dollar passes to the Super Bowl.

To reignite your relationship, you need to impersonate when you initially began dating, Orbuch said. One way to do that, is by engaging in a new activity or interest with your partner. Doing novel exercises with your accomplice empowers you to re experience the first profound state [at the start of your relationship]."

As such, taking a stab at something new starts fervor, creating enthusiasm. You can do anything from remote ocean fishing to salsa moving to climbing a mountain to eating at an alternate eatery.

12

Make New Recollections

Make New Recollections

The following stage is to deal with making new sure encounters together. "A positive encounter will move the energy for any couple," Beauchamp says. "Accomplish something that can make you snicker, grin, and reconnect in a positive way." Cook adds that these new recollections will impart trust in the relationship and remind the two accomplices that they are equipped for having blissful communications.

Use your abilities

Whether you are adroit at painting or cooking, you should utilize it and accomplish something particularly amazing for your partner. Cook something that's their favorite.

Else you can design your accomplice's room with some Do-It-Yourself techniques for an ideal sign of adoration. You can likewise perform something you are great at for them. A basic demonstration of adoration can do ponders. Make a consideration bundle for your partner

Make a consideration bundle for your partner and fill it with all their favorite items.

Incorporate natively constructed heated treats, most loved food sources, gift vouchers, books, adornments, pictures, and other most loved things. It will put a grin on your partners face and make them feel great inside. Plan time together to watch your partner open the consideration bundle or request that they make a video of opening the bundle and send it to you.

13

Spotlight on what's to come

Spotlight on what's to come

To abandon the previous you, both you and your partner should zero in on the thing that's coming down the road as opposed to harping on previous slip-ups. Beauchamp's recommendation is to have a transparent discussion about how you both need to push ahead into another period of your relationship. Plan a dream of your future together and how you maintain that it should be, and address both the present moment and long haul objectives.

14

Revamping trust as the person in question

Revamping TRUST AS THE Person in question

Remaking trust when you've been sold out

Having somebody break your trust can leave you feeling hurt, stunned, and, surprisingly, actually debilitated. It could provoke you to think about your relationship — and your partner — in another way.

If you have any desire to endeavor to reconstruct trust, here are a few decent beginning stages.

☐ Think about the purpose for the falsehood or disloyalty

At the point when you've been misled, you probably won't think often much about the explanations for it.

In some cases, individuals really do here and there lie when they just don't have the foggiest idea what else to do. This doesn't settle on their decision right, yet it can assist with thinking about how you could have responded in their situation.

Of course, your partner might have sold out you to safeguard themselves, yet they might have had an alternate thought process. Is it safe to say that they were attempting to shield you from terrible news? Make the best of a terrible cash circumstance? Help a relative?

Perhaps the treachery of trust came about because of a miscommunication or misconception.

Whatever occurred, it's essential to clarify that what they did wasn't alright. Yet, knowing the purposes for their activities might assist you with concluding whether you're ready to start modifying the trust you once shared.

☐ Impart, convey, convey
It very well may be excruciating or awkward, yet one of
the greatest parts of revamping trust after disloyalty is conversing with your accomplice about the circumstance.

Put away a chance to tell them obviously:

how you feel about the circumstance
why the selling out of trust hurt you
what you really want from them to begin reconstructing trust

Allow them an opportunity to talk, yet focus on their earnestness. Do they apologize and appear to be really remorseful? Or on the other hand would they say they are guarded and reluctant to take ownership of their disloyalty?

You might feel profound or upset during this discussion. These sentiments are totally substantial. In the event that you feel yourself lashing out to keep imparting in a useful manner, return a break and come to the subject later.

Discussing what happened is only the start. It's completely fine, and totally typical, on the off chance that you can't manage everything in an evening or two.

☐ Practice absolution

If you have any desire to fix a relationship after a selling out, pardoning is critical. Not exclusively will you want to pardon your accomplice, however you additionally may have to excuse yourself.

Faulting yourself here and there for what happened can keep you trapped in self-question. That can hurt the possibilities of your relationship's recuperation.

Contingent upon the treachery, it very well may be difficult to excuse your accomplice and push ahead. However, attempt to recall that generous your accomplice isn't saying that what they did was alright.

Rather, you're engaging yourself to find a sense of peace with what occurred and leave it previously. You're likewise allowing your accomplice an opportunity to gain and develop from their mix-ups.

☐ Try not to choose not to move on

When you've completely examined the double-crossing, it's by and large best to take care of the issue. This implies you would rather not bring it up in ongoing contentions.

You'll likewise need to back off of continually monitoring your accomplice to ensure they aren't deceiving you once more.

This is generally difficult, particularly from the beginning. You could struggle with relinquishing the disloyalty and find it challenging to begin confiding in your accomplice, particularly assuming you're stressed over another treachery.

In any case, when you choose to allow the relationship a subsequent opportunity, you're likewise choosing to trust your accomplice once more. Perhaps you can't totally believe them immediately, however you're inferring you'll allow trust an opportunity to regrow.

15

Potentially inquiries of the casualty wrongdoer

Potentially Inquiries OF THE Casualty Wrongdoer

☐ What about the details of an affair?

Relationship counselors often recommend against providing specific details about a sexual encounter with someone else. If you've cheated, your partner may have a lot of questions about what exactly happened. And you might want to answer them in an effort to be transparent.

But talking about the details of an encounter can cause further pain that isn't very productive. If your partner wants details, consider asking them to wait until you can see a therapist together.

The specialist can assist you with exploring the best method for resolving these inquiries. Meanwhile, you can in any case sincerely answer their inquiries without giving unequivocal subtleties.

☐ What amount of time will it require?

Being involved with broken trust can be incredibly awkward. The two sides may be anxious to get the entire reconstructing process over with as quick as could be expected. However, everything being equal, this takes time.

☐ How long, precisely? It relies upon a ton of elements, especially the occasion that broke the trust.

Well established examples of disloyalty or unscrupulously will take more time to determine. A solitary untruth grounded in a misconception or want to safeguard might be more straightforward to address, particularly when the accomplice who lied shows earnest lament and a restored obligation to correspondence.

Have persistence with yourself. Try not to allow your partner to rush you. A partner who really laments harming you might be harming, as well, yet to fix things, they ought to likewise comprehend it isn't useful to rush right once more into the status quo.

16

The bottom line

The bottom line

It's possible to rebuild a relationship after a breach of trust. Whether it's worth it depends on your relationship needs and whether you feel it's possible to trust your partner again.

If you do decide to try repairing things, be prepared for things to take some time. If both sides are committed to the process of rebuilding trust, you might find that you both come out stronger than before — both as a couple and on your own.

You've heard it a million times but it bears repeating: even the strongest relationships face challenges.

Building a happy, healthy partnership takes work and may not always be easy, especially when there's been a breach of trust. "Issues are a part of life and a part of being in a relationship," says clinical psychologist Stone Kraushaar. "And the goal is to not fixate on the past, but work to create together in a meaningful way."

17

Mostly asked questions

THE Casualty QUESTION

☐ Is it worth the effort?

Revamping trust is definitely not a simple undertaking. It's generally expected to address assuming it's even worth the effort before you choose to focus on dealing with your relationship.

On the off chance that your accomplice commits an error or two throughout the span of an involved acquaintance and takes ownership of it, dealing with trust issues might be the right move.

However long there's actually love and responsibility among you, chipping away at trust issues will just make your relationship more grounded.

Yet, in the event that you realize you'll at absolutely no point ever have the option to totally believe your accomplice in the future, regardless of what they do, it's for the most part best to make this clean straight up so you can both start to push ahead independently.

It's likewise worth gauging your choices assuming you've found long periods of treachery, monetary contemptibility, control, or other significant breaks of trust.

Other warnings that could flag now is the right time to call it quits include:

- proceeded with trickery or control
  - a deceitful expression of remorse
  - conduct that doesn't coordinate with their words

You don't need to do it single-handedly

Each relationship has a tough time. There's no disgrace in connecting for help.

Couples guiding can be an extraordinary asset while managing trust issues, especially those including disloyalty. An instructor can offer an impartial perspective on you relationship and assist the two partners with figuring out through fundamental problems.

Having extreme discussions about selling out and trust can likewise raise excruciating feelings on the two sides. Having a believed instructor can likewise assist you with exploring the troublesome sentiments as they emerge.

Made in the USA
Las Vegas, NV
05 January 2024